Celebrating your year

1951

a very special year for

First printed in 2020 in the USA (ISBN 979-8698686040). Revised in 2021, 2nd Edition (ISBN 978-0-6450623-1-1). Self-published through Kindle Direct Publishing and IngramSpark for Kid Hero Stories Pte. Ltd.

NUCLEAR BOMBS OVER NEVADA

CHURCHILL RETURNS TO POWER

THE KING AND I OPENING SUCCESS

Flashback to **1951** a very special year

FUNNY LADY LUCILLE BALL COMES TO TV

ROSENBERGS GUILTY

NAPALM DROPPED ON NORTH KOREA

INAUGURAL PAN AMERICAN GAMES

Let's flashback to 1951, a very special year.

Was this the year you were born?

Was this the year you were married?

Whatever the reason, this book is a celebration of your year,

THE YEAR 1951.

Turn the pages to discover a book packed with fun-filled fabulous facts. We look at the people, the places, the politics and the pleasures that made 1951 unique and helped shape the world we know today.

So get your time-travel suit on, and enjoy this trip down memory lane, to rediscover what life was like, back in the year 1951.

Career girl, 1965

Little Miss Telephone herself. Thirty-five members of her family have worked for the telephone company.

That's Karen Terry — She's just three and cute as a button. Already she's decided to be a telephone operator when she grows up.

There are many reasons for her choice. For Karen is related to an interesting telephone family in California. Thirty-five members of this family have worked for the telephone company in the past sixty-five years. Many still do.

Lots to Talk About — When Karen's Aunt Ella was asked what the dinner conversation is like when they get together, she said — "Why we talk shop, of course. All about the telephone company and our friends there."

It's that way with thousands of other families throughout the country. One Bell Telephone Company found that 2800, or ten per cent, of its employees had members of their families in telephone work.

Stepping Ahead — A young man doesn't follow his Dad in a job unless Dad says, "Come along, son — you'll find it as good a place as I did." You won't find sister following sister, and brother following brother into telephone work without reason. They like the work and the company.

Good people in good jobs help to give this country the best telephone service in the world at low cost.

BELL TELEPHONE SYSTEM

Career girl, 1965

Little Miss Telephone herself. Thirty-five members of her family have worked for the telephone company.

That's Karen Terry–She's just three and cute as a button. Already she's decided to be a telephone operator when she grows up.

There are many reasons for her choice. For Karen is related to an interesting telephone family in California. Thirty-five members of this family have worked for the telephone company in the past sixty-five years. Many still do.

Lots to Talk About–When Karen's Aunt Ella was asked what the dinner conversation is like when they get together, she said–"Why we talk shop, of course. All about the telephone company and our friends there."

It's that way with thousands of other families throughout the country. One Bell Telephone Company found that 2800, or ten per cent, of its employees had members of their families in telephone work.

Stepping Ahead–A young man doesn't follow his Dad in a job unless Dad says, "Come along, son–you'll find it as good a place as I did." You wont find sister following sister, and brother following brother into telephone work without reason. They like the work and the company.

Good people in good jobs help to give this country the best telephone service in the world at low cost.

Bell Telephone System

This advertisement first appeared in *Life Magazine* 12th Feb 1951.
It assumes the girl depicted would be a career girl by the time she is 17-years-old, in the year 1965.

Contents

1951 American Family Life

Imagine if time-travel was a reality, and one fine morning you wake up to find yourself flashed back in time, back to the year 1951.

What would life be like for a typical family, in a typical town, somewhere in America?

A family cooling off outside their home in the 1950s.

The post-war boom continued throughout the entire decade of the 50s, giving us booming birth numbers, booming suburbs, a booming economy, and the booming trappings of the consumerist culture we still enjoy today. With the stringent post-war years well behind us, the rising middle classes were feeling an urgent need to spend.

An unprecedented 3.75 million babies were born in 1951 (up from 2.8 million at the end of the war six years earlier).[1]

To cater to the increase in demand, new houses were built in record numbers, most of them in the new suburban developments springing up on the outskirts of towns. Home sales were boosted by returned soldiers who had access to low interest loans through the G.I. Bill (1944-1956). A house in the suburbs quickly became the American dream for white middle-class families.

Artist's impression of a family outing in 1950s America.

The family was everything. Fathers commuted to earn a salary. Wives were encouraged to quit their jobs and stay at home. Children walked to school and played outdoors in their well manicured gardens.

Families dined together, watched television together, and enjoyed leisure time and outings together.

The median family income was $3,700 [1] a year, unemployment was 3.1% and falling, with GDP at 8%.[2]

Average costs in 1951 [3]	
New house	$9,000
New car	$1,500
Vacuum cleaner	$15
Pop-up toaster	$21
A gallon of gas	$0.19

[1] census.gov/library/publications.html.
[2] thebalance.com/unemployment-rate-by-year-3305506 and thebalance.com/us-gdp-by-year-3305543.
[3] thepeoplehistory.com and mclib.info/reference/local-history-genealogy/historic-prices/.

Joining the television in our families' list of must-haves were: fully-automatic washing machines, front-loading dryers, defrost refrigerators, vacuum cleaners, air-conditioning and heating units, milkshake makers, and a multitude of other kitchen gadgets and home appliances. In addition we needed a family car or two, motorcycles, bicycles, hiking, camping, picnic gear, and much, much more.

An energetic and persuasive advertising industry, through TV, radio and print, ensured we always knew what our next purchase should be.

Drys Fresh...
Drys Fluffy...
...and takes only minutes in any weather

A Bendix automatic dryer advertisement from 1951.

An safety educational magazine from 1950.

ATOMIC BOMBING

HOW TO PROTECT YOURSELF

A Wise PUBLICATION

Prepared by Science Service, Inc.

But beneath the appearance of abundance and domestic bliss, Americans were deeply concerned. The Soviets had detonated an atomic bomb in 1949, setting in motion a nuclear race between the two superpowers–the Cold War.

By 1951 both powers were striving to build an even more powerful weapon–the hydrogen bomb.

We would endure another 40 years of tension between the two super-powers before the Cold War finally ended with the dissolution of the Soviet Union in 1991.

No other washer gives you such a perfect combination of washing advantages!

This is IT! The washer designed with YOU in mind... the 1951 Thor Spinner Washer with Hydro-Swirl Action! Four wonderful features are combined in this one wonderful washer! *Only Thor gives you all 4!*

Hydro-Swirl washing action! The Thor has it... the super-efficient Hydro-Swirl principle of washing. Thor lets the water do the work. It swishes and swirls clothes gently but thoroughly... actually washes clothes cleaner, faster, yet is safer for fabrics. And proved best by test in laboratory and home!

Saves 27 gallons of hot water! The 1951 Thor beats the 8 other leading automatic or semi-automatic washers in economy! Saves up to 27 gallons of hot water every washday for a family of 4! Proved by test! And Thor saves soap, saves fuel costs, too.

Controllable washing time! No fixed mechanical cycles that must be gone through. With the 1951 Thor, *you* decide how much water–*you* decided how long to wash each load. Then flick the switch. Thor washes and rinses, then spins your clothes damp dry–in one single tub! Your hands never touch hot, soapy water!

Thor-way overflow rinse! Look! Dirt and suds float up and off the top, *not down through the clothes*, as in ordinary washers. And the 1951 Thor has finger-tip control... lets you rinse (as well as wash) for as long or short a period as you like.

No Plumbing Installation Necessary! No Bolting Down! No Annoying Vibration!

Austerity in the United Kingdom

Now just imagine you flashed back to a town
in 1951 United Kingdom or Western Europe.

Unlike boom-time America, a very different,
more restrained lifestyle would await you.

London, like many other major European cities, bore the brunt of destruction from WWII bombings. Reconstruction was painfully slow, hampered by a general shortage of money, manpower and materials.

In cities there was a desperate shortage of housing to accommodate the growing population. Nearly half of those in cities lived in private, rented, often substandard apartments. While in the country, homes often lacked water, sanitation, electricity and phones.

A London street scene in 1950.

Stifling and miserable austerity measures, in place since the start of the war, were slowly being lifted. By 1951, most items were available for purchase without coupons, however rationing of meat and sugar would continue for a few more years.

The post-war baby boom, along with the shortage of funds and building materials for new schools, often resulted in crowded classes of up to 50 students in urban areas.

British children at school in the early 50s.

Snap elections held in October 1951, just 20 months after the February 1950 elections, saw the ruling Labour Party lose to the Conservatives. Winston Churchill, UK Prime Minister from 1940-1945, would be reinstalled for an additional four years from 1951-1955.

Within months, Churchill traveled to the USA for talks with President Truman, with the aim of renewing UK's "special relationship" with America, and to discuss joint strategies for communism containment.

Cuts 92% of your driving motions! New Fordomatic Drive does your gear shifting for you. It's America's newest, finest, most flexible automatic transmission!

Stretch your driving dollars—with Ford's Automatic Mileage Maker! You get high-compression performances with regular gasoline! A new Waterproof Ignition System prevents engine "shorts" from moisture.

No car is better finished, better built! There's quality that lasts in the quiet elegance of Ford's new Luxury Lounge interior, in the soundness of Ford's coachwork!

Enjoy "Fashion-Car" styling—from the new recessed headlights to new Jet-Styled Windsplits. Ford's designed to stay "right" in the years ahead!

Feel the safety of an extra-heavy steel Luxury Lifeguard Body! And Ford's new Double-Seal King-Size Brakes keep out dirt and water—give smooth, safe stops in any weather!

"Test Drive" the '51 Ford... at your Ford Dealer's today. And as your drive it, remember that this car is built for the years ahead! With 43 "Look Ahead" features, it was planned and engineered to stay young in performance, to stay in style, to stay thrifty—for years to come!

Relax with Ford's new Automatic Ride Control! It adjusts your ride to any road automatically! The going stays easy, level—no pitch, no jounce, no roll!

Our Love Affair with Cars

In the short few years since war's end, the US car industry had shifted from fabricating utilitarian war tanks and trucks, to producing fashionable consumer vehicles, the kind of which we just had to have.

There were now 42.5 million registered cars on US roads, up from 25 million at war's end.[1] Our love affair with cars was firmly entrenched.

Cars on a Philadelphia traffic circle in the early 50s.

Detroit had long been the car manufacturing hub of the country, and America led the world in car production, turning out 7.2 million vehicles in 1951 alone. This equated to more than 80% of all new vehicles worldwide.[1]

With a population of 1.85 million people, Detroit had become the 4th largest city in the US.[2] And by the end of the decade, a whopping one in six adults nation-wide would be employed in the car industry.

[1] fhwa.dot.gov/ohim/summary95/mv200.pdf.
[2] theweek.com/articles/461968/rise-fall-detroit-timeline.

Our love affair with cars grew hand-in-hand with the post-war baby boom and housing construction boom. Where would we be without our cars? How else could we get from our far-flung suburban homes to our inner city offices?

Now-get the Plus of a Packard at the price of a car!

Studebaker again amazes America!

Above–1951 Packard Patrician 400.

Left–1951 Studebaker Commander.

Rising incomes ensured the family car was increasingly affordable. An additional 2.4 million vehicles were put on the US roads as families fled the cities for the quiet life of the suburbs.

1951 Hudson Step-down.

Cars were no longer just a necessity; they had become an expression of our personality. Sturdy, sporty, or luxurious, cars now came in a wide range of styles, colors, and price points, with chrome, wings, stripes and fins for added personality.

From the stitches in its seats to the head bolts on its power plant, Mercury is *precision-built* for the years ahead of it. For long-run investment, you're smart to put your money in this penny-pincher!

Mercury stays new longer—keeps upkeep low and trade-in value high—goes easy on gas—gives you what you want and deserve from a 1951 car.

You get a great new car that *looks* the part. There's a sweep of motion in its line and a sense of power in its look. But *Mercury's* beauty goes far deeper than that—it's built into every part of the car!

Drive a Mercury first chance you get. Test the whisper-hustle of its great 8-cylinder, V-type engine. Check the broader, softer seating—the new increased visibility—the extra roominess. Then you be the judge.

You'll decide Mercury's got what you want—and you'll enjoy it for many years to come!

RCA Victor Million Proof television–proven in over a million homes

They "look like a million"–and they're Million Proof–the new RCA Victor television
receivers!

Any one you choose gives you the best in picture quality, styling and performance. And
no wonder! They're built from RCA Victor's experience in producing *well over a million*
television receivers.

All have the new, extra-powerful RCA Victor circuits for peak performance. The
fabulous RCA Victor television pick-up brings in the picture even in "fringe" areas. All
have the rich, true-to-life tone of RCA Victor's famous "Golden Throat" acoustical system.
All have decorator cabinets–styled to "live with" the finest of modern or traditional
furnishings.

And–*only* when you buy RCA Victor television can you buy the RCA Victor Factory-
Service Contract for expert installation and maintenance.

The Golden Age of Television

The television set quickly became the centerpiece of every family home. By 1951, 10.3 million American households, equivalent to 23.5% of the population, owned a television set, (an increase from 3.88 million households, or just 9% of the population 12 months earlier).[1] And that number would rise exponentially throughout the decade as television became our preferred choice of entertainment.

Family focussed Motorola television advertisements from 1951.

For the rising middle classes, television was much more convenient than going to a downtown cinema. It provided an increasing array of programs to watch, it was available every day of the week, and it was free to watch once purchased.

[1] americancentury.omeka.wlu.edu/items/show/136.

Most Popular Television Shows of 1951

1	Arthur Godfrey's Talent Scouts	11	Mama
2	Texaco Star Theater	12	Philco TV Playhouse
3	I Love Lucy	13	Amos 'n' Andy
4	The Red Skelton Show	14	Gangbusters
5	The Colgate Comedy Hour	15	Big Town
6	Arthur Godfrey and His Friends	16	Goodyear TV Playhouse
7	Fireside Theatre	17	Pabst Blue Ribbon Bouts
8	Your Show of Shows	18	The Lone Ranger
9	The Jack Benny Show	19	Gillette Cavalcade of Sports
10	You Bet Your Life	20	All Star Revue
		=	Dragnet

* From the Nielsen Media Research 1951-52 season of top-rated primetime television series.

In the early 50s television continued to rely on live broadcasts of popular radio programs, as these were faster to produce, and cheaper than new made-for-TV dramas.

Comedy-Varieties remained our most popular form of family-time TV entertainment, accounting for six of the top eight programs for the year.

Dean Martin and Jerry Lewis in
The Colgate Comedy Hour (NBC. 1950-1955).

Also keeping us glued to our screens were highly rated drama series such as *Fireside Theater* (NBC. 1949-58), *Philco TV Playhouse* (NBC. 1948-55), *Goodyear TV Playhouse* (NBC. 1951-57), and *The Lone Ranger* (ABC. 1949-57).

Clayton Moore and Jay Silverheels in
The Lone Ranger (ABC. 1949-1957).

Jack Webb in *Dragnet* (NBC. 1951-70, Syndication. 1989-91, ABC. 2003-04).

Lynn Loring and Mary Stuart in *Search for Tomorrow* (CBS. 1951-82, NBC. 1982-86).

The television networks were quick to turn out new programs to keep us tuning in. Here are just a few of the new programs that aired for the first time in 1951: *Dragnet, The Red Skelton Show, Search for Tomorrow (35 seasons), I Love Lucy, Hallmark Hall of Fame, What's My Line* (UK), and *Crazy People* (UK).

Red Skelton in *The Red Skelton Show* (NBC. 1951-1971).

Peter Sellers, Harry Secombe, Spike Milligan, & Michael Bentine, in *Crazy People* (later *The Goons*, BBC. 1951-60).

Telechron can't run wrong!

ELECTRIC CLOCKS   AND THEY START AT $4.50*

IVY Perfect gift to grace her kitchen. Hangs on wall or sets on shelf. Takes real vines in twin vases color-styled in red, grey, green, yellow. **$7.95***

AIRLUX Gift of elegance. For bedroom, mantel, desk. Rich hand-rubbed mahogany finish case. Bell alarm. **$17.50***

Telechron electric clocks are silent. Need no winding, oiling, regulating. Choose from 29 lovely models for every room in the house. Full-year written warranty. Famous Telechron Synchro-Sealed Motor is synchronized perfectly with electric power plants so it has to run right! Telechron is a trademark of Telechron Inc., Ashland, Mass., a General Electric Affiliate.

*Prices and specifications subject to change. Prices plus existing tax.

Telechron Electric Clocks can't run wrong! And they start at $4.50

Ivy. Perfect gift to grace her kitchen. Hangs on wall or sets on shelf. Takes real vines in twin vases color-styled in red, grey, green, yellow. $7.95.

Airlux. Gift of elegance. For bedroom, mantel, desk. Rich hand-rubbed mahogany finish case. Bell alarm. $17.50.

Telechron electric clocks are silent. Need no winding, oiling, regulating. Choose from 29 lovely models for every room in the house. Full-year written warranty. Famous Telechron Synchro-Sealed Motor is synchronized perfectly with electric power plants so it has to run right!

Everybody Loves Lucy

In mid-October 1951, Lucille Ball launched onto our screens and into our hearts as New York housewife Lucy Ricardo, along-side real-life husband Desi Arnaz, in the sitcom *I Love Lucy*.

Spanning six seasons, the groundbreaking sitcom was the first scripted television program to be filmed in front of a live television audience. It would become the most watched TV show in 4 out of its 6-year run. Three film cameras allowed for multiple angle capture of every scene, a standard technique still used in sitcom production today.

Lucille Ball with Desi Arnaz.

Ball continued her comedic genius for CBS with *The Lucille Ball-Desi Arnaz Show* (1957-1960), *The Lucy Show* (1962-1968), and *Here's Lucy* (1968-1974). In 1986, ABC aired the 8 episode *Life with Lucy*.

The cast of *I Love Lucy*: William Frawley, Desi Arnaz, Vivian Vance and Lucille Ball.

The main cast in an episode from 1955.

A total of 180 half-hour *I Love Lucy* episodes were filmed, still watched around the world today as re-runs.

I Love Lucy holds the honor of being the first TV show to be inducted into the *Television Academy Hall of Fame* (1951).

In 2012 the show was ranked the Best TV Comedy and the Best TV Show in *Best in TV: The Greatest TV Shows of Our Time*.

But for him... words would be sterile, meaningless things... words like freedom, liberty, justice, equality... words that make pacts, proclamations, constitutions, charters... hopes for a better, more peaceful future.

Back of each man with a gun there are at least 25 men in uniform. They are men who are doers in their own right... specialists in communications, transportation, engineering, food, housing, motors, maintenance, repairs, electronics and many others.

Today's Army is a multiple combination of teams... in which all individuals merge their identity for a cause. Yet, as on any team in civilian life, individuals emerge from the group to carry the team and the cause.

Your Army is constantly seeking individuals of courage and initiative. Last year more than 200,000 men volunteered for the role of HIM. If you believe you can qualify, stop in at your nearest U.S. Army and U.S. Air Force Recruiting Station and see how much your Army offers you!

American forces entered the Korean War in June 1950, to assist South Korea with expelling Communist invaders from the north. By the start of 1951, the South Korean, US and UN forces were exhausted from the relentless battles against the powerful North Korean military (KPA).

While the Allies fought for a return to the Post War status quo of two Koreas divided along the 38th Parallel, the KPA was determined to unite Korea as one country under communist rule.

Crew of an M24 tank along the Naktong River front, 24th August 1950.

Soldiers take cover behind a tank during an attack. Hongchon area, 22nd May 1951.

With financial backing from the Soviets and China, the KPA first captured Seoul in June 1950, holding the capital for 3 months before being pushed back northwards to the border with China.

Chinese forces entered the war in large numbers at the end of 1950, joining the KPA to push south and recapture Seoul. January to April 1951 saw the Chinese launch their Third, Fourth and Fifth Offensives in quick succession on the embattled southern divisions.

In contrast to the well equipped and well trained KPA, the South Korean military forces were ill prepared and outnumbered.

US supplied machinery and artillery took several months to obtain. As fresh US Army and Marine Corps units arrived, they brought with them much needed tanks, antiaircraft guns, rocket launchers, jets and bombers.

An F4U-4B Corsair of Squadron 113 (VF-113) flies over US ships at Inchon, 15th Sept 1950.

A Hawker Sea Fury FB.11 fighter from British aircraft carrier HMS Glory, 1st June 1951.

Joining the war effort were a UN combined force from twenty-one countries including the UK, Australia, Canada, France, Philippines, and Thailand.

Outnumbered on the ground, the UN forces exploited their superior air power, dominating the skies in the early months of the war.

Air combat quickly became deadlier as Chinese and Soviet jet fighters took up battle. US pilots conducted night-time bomb raids, venturing deeper and deeper into North Korea to destroy enemy targets.

A total of 635,000 tons of bombs were dropped on North Korea, turning nearly every city and village to rubble. Citizens were advised to dig tunnels to live in.

In addition, the US dropped 32,557 tons of lethal napalm.

A US Air Force Fighter Bomber releases two napalm bombs over industrial military targets in North Korea, Jan 1951.

Medical corpsmen helping wounded infantrymen, following the fight for Hill 598, 14th Oct 1952.

A grief-stricken infantryman whose buddy had been killed in action, Haktong-ni area, 28th Aug 1950.

Korean girl with baby brother on her back walks by a stalled M-46 tank at Haengju, 9th June 1950.

The city of Seoul was captured 4 times during the first 12 months of battle. Casualties of war saw the population shrink from 1.5 million inhabitants pre-war, to around 200,000.

Food shortages and lack of housing were severe.

An estimated 3 million people lost their lives during the war, of which half were civilians from both South and North Korea. Causes of death included bombings, massacres, starvation and disease.

The war unofficially ended in July 1953 with the creation of the Demilitarized Zone separating the two Koreas. To date no peace treaty has been signed, leaving the two Koreas technically still at war.

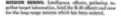

Bombs Away!

That terse report from bombardier to aircraft commander on the B-50 intercom means: "Mission accomplished!" It marks the climax of a Strategic Air Command mission... pushed through by men with guts, despite enemy flack and fighters. It means another blow at the enemy's power to strike.

As the bombardier speaks, all across the formation bombs slant toward the earth, five weather-dark miles below, pulled forward by the 450-mile-an-hour speed of the giant aircraft. This is the moment of climax.

But back of that dramatic moment is a long history of planning and preparation. Top-notch design... top-flight training... and the raw courage of men who make your U.S. Air Force the best in the world.

Top Aviation Cadet training produced this B-50 team's Aircraft Commander and Pilot... taught Navigator, Bombardier and Radar Officer to work interchangeably in one another's jobs. Great Air Force schools trained the Airman crew... flight engineer, radio operator, central fire control man, gunner-electrician.

And, behind them all... the vast organization of your modern Air Force has worked toward that moment of climax. Radar, radio maintenance, weather, intelligence... all pointed for that report by the bombardier: "BOMBS AWAY!"

The Nevada Proving Grounds were established in 1951 for the explicit purpose of testing nuclear devices. The Grounds covered 1,360 square miles of desert and mountain terrain in Nevada, Las Vegas.

Operation Buster-Jangle was the first US nuclear field exercise conducted on land. Troops observed the blast from 6 miles away, 1st Nov 1951.

Commencing on 27th January, a series of 5 bombs were dropped from B-50D bombers and exploded in open air. Over the next 41 years, a total of 1,021 nuclear tests would be carried out here. Of these, 100 were atmospheric tests, before underground testing became the norm.

Mushroom clouds from atmospheric tests could be seen from Las Vegas, leading to an increase in tourism. Hotels promoted mushroom cloud viewing parties, advertising the detonation times for advanced bookings.

It is estimated that millions of Americans were unwittingly exposed to the radioactive iodine fallout from the bombs.

Las Vegas postcard from 1951.

The Red Scare and the Rosenbergs

In the early 50s, American politicians repeatedly warned the public to be fearful of the Communist influence. Communists could be lurking anywhere, living and working among us, aiding the Soviets in their quest for world domination. During 1951 this paranoia reached new heights when Julius and Ethel Rosenberg were convicted of spying for the Soviets.

Julius and Ethel Rosenberg, separated by heavy wire screen as they leave US Court House after being found guilty by jury, 1951.

Julius Rosenberg was accused of leading a network of spies, several of whom had been arrested a year earlier on suspicion of passing top-secret information to the Soviets. This information included American designs on the construction of nuclear weapons.

His wife was accused of assisting in her husband's spy network.

The trial of the Rosenbergs in March 1951 lasted just three weeks. They were found guilty of espionage and condemned to die in the electric chair, making them the only two American civilians to be executed for espionage-related activity during the Cold War.

Documents released decades later proved Ethel Rosenberg's role in her husband's activities were minor and limited. Her conviction and execution were wrongful. She had been framed by her brother and sister-in-law, who were themselves spies in the same network.

Churchill Returns to Power

The British general election of October 1951 saw Winston Churchill's Conservative Party return to power with a slim majority of seats, despite not winning the popular vote. It marked the start of a 13-year rule by the Conservatives. Churchill, 76 years old, would remain in power a further four years, resigning in 1955 due to health concerns.

During this period Churchill made four trips to America. Although on good terms with both President Truman and later President Eisenhower, the Americans knew the Empire was in decline, and did not wholly support Churchill's commitment to ongoing British imperialism.

Churchill was UK Prime Minister from 1940-1945 and 1951-1955. He led the Conservative Party for 15 years (having led the Liberal Party for 20 years earlier).

Churchill with Americans General (later President) Dwight D. Eisenhower and Field Marshal Bernard Law Montgomery, 19th October 1951.

Churchill had served as an army officer and war correspondent in British India, Anglo-Sudan and the Second Boer Wars. He was also a writer, receiving a Nobel Prize for Literature in 1953.

Churchill is remembered as a great war-time leader.

Churchill wearing Garter robes, with his son and grandson standing behind.

Chinese Rule Over Tibet

After months of Chinese military occupation, delegates from the Buddhist mountain nation of Tibet were summoned to Beijing to negotiate a peace deal. They were then presented with a document known as the *Seventeen Point Agreement for the Peaceful Liberation of Tibet*, which was duly signed on 23rd May 1951. Under the terms of the Agreement, Tibet now officially belonged to China.

The Peoples Liberation Army of China marching into Lhasa, Tibet, 26th October 1951.

The Chinese government claimed that Tibet was always a part of China. However Tibet's government-in-exile maintains their representatives were forced to sign the Agreement, rendering it invalid.

Tenzin Gyatso, Tibet's 14th Dalai Lama in New Delhi, India, 1956.

Chinese rule included socialist land reforms, public humiliations, torture, suppression of religion, and military crackdowns over any resistance.

During the decade, Tibetan resistance guerrillas, with financial support from the CIA, fought against Chinese occupation. Tibetan exiles claim that more than one million have died at the hands of the Chinese since 1951.

During 1959, fearing for his life, Tibet's spiritual leader—the Dalai Lama—fled to India.

Apartheid Laws in South Africa

The Afrikaner National Party of South Africa came to power in 1948 with "apartheid" (apartness) as their slogan and political goal. White supremacist laws were immediately enacted to reinforce white minority rule and divide non-whites along color and tribal lines. The following years saw numerous Acts come into effect, to strengthen the apartheid rule.

The creation of the *Group Areas Act* (1950) and the *Prevention of Illegal Squatting Act* (1951) ensured 80% of the land was reserved for exclusive ownership by the ruling white minority.

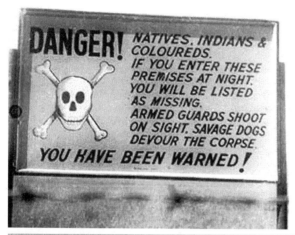

These Acts allowed for forcible, often violent, removal of non-whites from white designated areas. Evictions of entire suburbs, destruction of property, fines and criminal arrests became commonplace over the following years.

Area warning signs were commonplace.

The voting rights of blacks and mixed-race were removed with the *Separate Representation of Voters Act* (1951). Interracial marriage or sex was prohibited. Access to schools and other facilities were separately designated. Even access to employment was controlled. The Native Building Workers Act (1951) allowed for Blacks to access training for certain types of semi-skilled jobs but limited the areas they were permitted to work.

Protest marches and police action in South Africa in the early 50s.

These Acts were strengthened and amended multiple times over subsequent years.

Following decades of international condemnation and sanctions, the laws were finally repealed in 1991 with the dismantling of South Africa's Apartheid system.

Grandma leads a fast life... and loves it!

No one has to go home to see Grandma today because now *she's* going... by Skyliner. Age simply doesn't matter. From the moment she settles in her comfortable seat until the family waves hello, Grandma is in good hands. A thoughtful TWA hostess is always nearby, anticipating every need. And best of all, TWA's direct routes across the U.S. end any worries about changing places or transferring baggage. It's easy and fun traveling TWA–for *all ages*. Grandmas love it!

Where in the world do you want to go? For flight information and reservations call TWA or your travel agent.

Across the U.S. and overseas... you can depend on TWA

Hollywood's lovely young **SALLY FORREST** co-starring in Metro-Goldwyn-Mayer's *"BANNERLINE"*

Sally Forrest's silky-soft golden hair ripples with sparkling waves. See how lovely Rayve Creme Shampoo makes your hair—how easy to curl!

Young Hollywood stars agree that

No other shampoo makes your hair so shining clean... so easy to curl!

The absolutely perfect shampoo—that's what Hollywood's young beauties have christened Rayve Creme Shampoo! They adore the sparkling new highlights . . . the soft, fresh beauty of Rayve-clean hair. And Rayve leaves your hair so soft and lively—just ready to fall into nice deep waves!

Now—see the new beauty Rayve gives your hair! Fresh and shining, gloriously clean, dancing with light . . . eager to curl! Rayve's unique balanced formula combines *deep-cleansing* lather with rich *curl-conditioning* oils . . . coaxes out shining new-found waves and curls you never *dreamed* you had.

The limp wave test will show you! Give yourself a Rayve Creme Shampoo at the very *end* of your permanent—when your wave's all but gone! You'll see how Rayve revives your wave—washes new sparkle into your hair. Get a tube or jar of Rayve Creme Shampoo today . . . and see how it makes even a tired wave just *want* to curl!

MONEY-BACK GUARANTEE! If your Rayve-clean hair isn't shinier . . . softer . . . curlier . . . send Rayve carton or cap-liner with name and address to Rayve, Box 2, 505 Park Avenue, N. Y. Full purchase price refunded immediately!

Young Hollywood stars agree that

No other shampoo makes your hair so shining clean... so easy to curl.

The absolutely perfect shampoo–that's what Hollywood's young beauties have christened Rayve Creme Shampoo! They adore the sparkling new highlights... the soft, fresh beauty of Rayve-clean hair. And Rayve leaves your hair so soft and lively–just ready to fall into nice deep waves!

Now–see the new beauty Rayve gives your hair! Fresh and shining, gloriously clean, dancing with light... eager to curl! Rayve's unique balanced formula combines *deep-cleaning* lather with rich *curl-conditioning* oils... coaxes out shining new-found waves and curls you never *dreamed* you had.

The limp wave test will show you! Give yourself a Rayve Creme Shampoo at the very *end* of your permanent–when your wave's all but gone! You'll see how Rayve revives your wave–washes new sparkle into your hair. Get a tube or jar of Rayve Creme Shampoo today... and see how it makes even a tired wave just *want* to curl!

1951 in Cinema and Film

Scene from *Quo Vadis* (MGM. 1951).

Highest Paid Stars

1 John Wayne
2 Dean Martin
= Jerry Lewis
4 Betty Grable
5 Bud Abbott
= Lou Costello

Having reached its peak in the mid 1940's, cinema attendance faced a steady decline throughout the 1950s. With more and more families filling their leisure time with the convenience of television, the motion-picture industry sought new ways to win over new audiences.

Younger audiences now had cash to spare. Movie themes adjusted to accommodate the new trends in popular culture, and to exploit the sex appeal status of young, rising stars such as Marilyn Monroe, James Dean and Marlon Brando.

Dean Martin, Jerry Lewis and Marilyn Monroe at the 1953 Redbook Awards.

Grace Kelly in 1951.

1951 film debuts

Jeff Bridges	The Company She Keeps
Charles Bronson	You're in the Navy Now
Leslie Caron	An American in Paris
Grace Kelly	Fourteen Hours
Leonard Nimoy	Queen for a Day
William Shatner	The Butler's Night Off

* From en.wikipedia.org/wiki/1951_in_film.

Top Grossing Films of the Year

1	Quo Vadis	MGM	$11,143,000
2	Show Boat	MGM	$5,293,000
3	David and Bathsheba	20th Century Fox	$4,720,000
4	The Great Caruso	MGM	$4,309,000
5	A Streetcar Named Desire	Warner Bros.	$4,250,000
6	The African Queen	United Artists	$4,100,000
7	That's My Boy	Paramount	$3,800,000
8	An American in Paris	MGM	$3,750,000
9	A Place in the Sun	Paramount	$3,500,000
10	Father's Little Dividend	MGM	$3,122,000

* From en.wikipedia.org/wiki/1951_in_film by box office gross in the USA.

MGM's musical comedy *An American in Paris* won seven of its nine nominations.

The lavish historical epic *Quo Vadis* was the run-away box office success of the year, bringing in over $11 million in US ticket sales and nearly as much at the foreign box offices. The film was nominated for eight Academy Awards, but failed to win any.

The Day the Earth Stood Still by 20th Century Fox.

The Man from Planet X by United Artists.

Flight to Mars by Monogram.

When Worlds Collide by Paramount.

A Streetcar Named Desire

Vivien Leigh as Blanche DuBois in *A Streetcar Named Desire* (Warner Bros. 1951).

Based on Tennessee Williams' 1947 Pulitzer Prize-winning play, the 1951 film version of *A Streetcar Named Desire* cast Marlon Brando, Kim Hunter, and Karl Malden in their original Broadway roles. The lead role for heroine Blanche duBois was given to Vivien Leigh, who previously played the role in London's West End.

Brando was a relatively unknown actor at the time of casting. He received his first Oscar nomination for his performance.

Cinema poster from 1951.

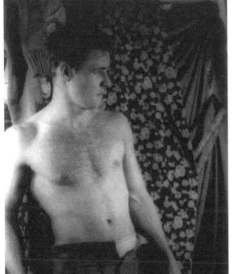

The controversial themes tackled in the play—suicide, homosexuality, and rape—were largely ignored or lightly passed over in the movie, in order to conform to the Motion Picture Production Code.

A Streetcar Named Desire has since been preserved by the US Library of Congress National Film Registry.

Marlon Brando portrait from the Broadway theatre production *A Streetcar Named Desire*, 1948.

"RC makes you feel like new!" says Gene Tierney

Whenever I feel tired RC makes me feel like new! Yes, and I know Royal Crown Cola tastes best, too. For I compared leading colas, in an impartial taste-test, and RC won my vote! Gene Tierney.

See me in "On the Riviera"
a 20th Century-Fox Picture.
Color by Technicolor.

Smart girls want the best . . .

Of course, you choose clothes that bring out your best points . . . whether it's a dinner date or a day at the office.

Why not take the same angle towards your office typewriter?

Decide on the new Royal Electric. It brings out your best points as an up-and-coming secretary. It was designed with you in mind.

The Royal Electric Typewriter is newly designed throughout, so that electricity does the work for you! Tension and fatigue are well-nigh banished . . . and you *feel* better and *look* better, when five o'clock rolls around.

And what a joy to operate! The controls are in the same positions as on your favorite Royal Standard Typewriter. There's virtually no "change-over" problem. What a break to be on familiar ground.

Now, you ask, how about the work? It pours out . . . literally. As many as 20 carbon copies, too. Your letters sparkle with a crisp clarity that does you credit. Heavy-duty work is delivered with remarkable speed and efficiency.

Exclusive "Touch Control" allows you to adjust the touch to give you the "feel" you prefer. Exclusive "Magic" Margin permits instant, automatic margin setting.

The Royal Electric is *your* typewriter . . . because of its many exclusive features . . . because it was designed with *you* in mind. So— choose the finest. Choose Royal.

ROYAL Electric Typewriter

Smart girls want the best...
Of course, you choose clothes that bring out your best point... whether it's a dinner date or a day at the office.

Why not take the same angle toward your office typewriter?

Decide on the new Royal Electric. It brings out your best points as an up-and-coming secretary. It was designed with you in mind.

The Royal Electric Typewriter is newly designed throughout, so that electricity does the work for you! Tension and fatigue are well-nigh banished... and you *feel* better and *look* better, when five o'clock rolls around.

And what a joy to operate! The controls are in the same positions as on your favorite Royal Standard Typewriter. There's virtually no "change-over" problem. What a break to be on familiar ground.

Now, you ask, how about the work? It pours out... literally. As many as 20 carbon copies, too. Your letters sparkle with a crisp clarity that does you credit. Heavy-duty work is delivered with remarkable speed and efficiency.

Exclusive "Touch Control" allows you to adjust the touch to give you the "feel" you prefer. Exclusive "Magic" Margin permits instant, automatic margin setting.

The Royal Electric is *your* typewriter... because of its many exclusive features... because it was designed with *you* in mind. So–choose the finest. Choose Royal.

The King and I Broadway Triumph

Gertrude Lawrence and Yul Brynner pose in full costume for *The King and I* original stage production.

The King and I opened on Broadway's St. James Theatre on 29th March 1951 to triumphant reviews. It would run for 3 years, winning Tony Awards for Best Musical, Best Actress (Gertrude Lawrence) and Best Featured Actor (Yul Brynner). The crowd pleaser was later made into a film (1956), continued with a national tour, and saw numerous stage revivals.

Oscar Hammerstein (standing) with Richard Rodgers (at the piano).

The King and I was the fifth musical by successful musical theatre team Richard Rogers (composer) and Oscar Hammerstein (lyricist). The duo were not so much concerned *if* the film would be a success, but rather if it would be a bigger success then their earlier sensation *South Pacific* (1949).

Brynner was a young newcomer when he first appeared on stage as King Mongkut in the original 1951 production. He reprised his role for the 1954 touring production, the 1977 and 1985 Broadway revivals, as well as the 1979 London production. In total Brynner played the King on stage 4,625 times.

Brynner also won an Oscar for his role in the 1956 film version of *The King and I.*

Brynner poses as the King of Siam for the CBS television series *Anna and the King*, 1972.

Lawrence and Brynner on stage for the original production of *The King and I*, 1951.

The musical continues to enthrall audiences today, having undergone a major reworking in Christopher Renshaw's 1991 Australian production. Renshaw reworked sets, costumes, and dance sequences to express a more authentic Thai experience, including all Asian performers in the Asian roles. He believed the original version was now seen as culturally insensitive and sought to create a more politically correct version. This modern version went on to win four Tony Awards for its 1996 Broadway revival, including the *Best Revival* award.

1951 Billboard Top 30 Songs

	Artist	Song Title
1	Nat King Cole	Too Young
2	Tony Bennett	Because of You
3	Les Paul & Mary Ford	How High the Moon
4	Rosemary Clooney	Come on-a My House
5	Mario Lanza	Be My Love
6	The Weavers	On Top of Old Smoky
7	Tony Bennett	Cold, Cold Heart
8	Perry Como	If
9	Mario Lanza	The Loveliest Night of the Year
10	Patti Page	Tennessee Waltz

Nat King Cole

Tony Bennett

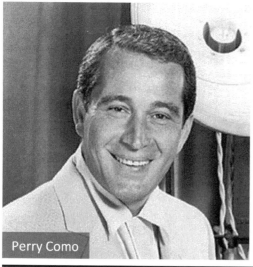

Perry Como

Patti Page

	Artist	Song Title
11	Frankie Laine	Jezebel
12	Tony Martin	I Get Ideas
13	Les Paul & Mary Ford	Mockin' Bird Hill
14	Patti Page	Mockin' Bird Hill
15	Guy Mitchell & Mitch Miller	My Heart Cries for You
16	Eddy Howard	(It's No) Sin
17	Vaughn Monroe	Sound Off
18	Dinah Shore	Sweet Violets
19	Les Paul & Mary Ford	The World Is Waiting for the Sunrise
20	Guy Mitchell & Mitch Miller	My Truly, Truly Fair

Dinah Shore in 1951.

Debbie Reynolds in 1954.

	Artist	Song Title
21	The Four Aces	(It's No) Sin
22	Debbie Reynolds & Carleton Carpenter	Aba Daba Honeymoon
23	Frankie Laine	Rose, Rose, I Love You
24	Del Wood	Down Yonder
25	Billy Eckstine	I Apologize
26	Patti Page	Would I Love You
27	Perry Como & The Fontane Sisters	You're Just in Love
28	Ames Brothers with The Les Brown Orchestra	Undecided
29	Phil Harris	The Thing
30	Les Baxter	Because of You

* From the *Billboard* top 30 singles of 1951.

Mrs. Humphrey Bogart (Laruen Bacall) says

Lauren Bacall, speaking for style-wise women everywhere, endorses The New Idea in Smoking from the feminine point of view... As for men, they go in a big way for delicious smoking pleasure in a shape, trim and handy as a cigarette... The *perfect mild* smoke.

Convenient as a cigarette... Fits neatly between the smoker's lips, or into a holder.

Humphrey Bogart and his wife, Lauren Bacall, co-stars of Santana Pictures, are both ardent, expert sailors.

Greek athlete Aristeidis Roubanis lighting the cauldron to commence the Games, 1951.

Buenos Aires, Argentina, was the host city for the first Pan American Games in 1951.

The Games were originally proposed decades earlier by Latin American representatives of the Olympics, but the Second World War caused plans to be shelved.

The Games opened with the lighting of the cauldron with a flame from Greece, sent by the International Olympic Committee.

18 sports were offered, bringing together 2,513 participants from 14 nations. Canada did not attend but joined in later games.

Argentina won a total of 142 medals of which 63 were Gold. The USA came second with 101 medals including 46 Gold.

Chile, Cuba, Brazil and Mexico all performed well, bringing home multiple medals each.

Poster for the 1951 Pan American Games.

Billed as an Olympic-style Summer competition for athletes from all the Americas, the Games are held every four years, always one year before the Olympic Games. More than 40 nations took part in the most recent Games.

Cover of *Mundo Deportivo* magazine, 15th March 1951.

If suits of clothes were worn only once and then thrown away, like paper napkins, there might be some justification for buying the cheapest. But a suit must have a future.

It must stand up to the rigors of life and also give evidence of your good taste every time you wear it. That's why so many well-dressed men look for the *Trumpeter** label before they look for the price tag. The label is their guarantee of fine tailoring and lasting quality. The price (so often less than you expect!) is as low as that quality permits.

A Palette Tone Diagonal (shown above in a patch-pocket model) is always in quiet, good taste.

HART SCHAFFNER & MARX*

If suits of clothes were worn only once and then thrown away, like paper napkins, there might be some justification for buying the cheapest. But a suit must have a future.

It must stand up to the rigors of life and also give evidence of your good taste every time you wear it. That's why so many well-dressed men look for the *Trumpeter** label before they look for the price tag. The label is their guarantee of fine tailoring and lasting quality. The price (so often less than you expect!) is as low as that quality permits.

Other Sporting Events from 1951

5th Apr– Ben Hogan won his first US Golf Masters Tournament. During his golfing career he would claim nine major championships and be inducted into the World Golf Hall of Fame in 1971.

5th Sep– 16-year-old Maureen Connolly Brinker won her first grand slam title at the US Open. The US teenager would prove to be one of tennis' greats, winning nine grand slams, including a golden slam in 1953. In 1954, at age 19, a horseback riding injury ended her tennis career.

10th Sep– American Florence Chadwick became the first woman to swim the English Channel in both directions.

16th Sep– American Betsy Rawls won the first of her 8 major titles at the US Women's Open, Druid Hills Golf Club, in Atlanta, Georgia.

26th Oct– Underdog Rocky Marciano defeated former champion Joe Louis by TKO in the 8th round at Madison Square Garden. He would hold the title of heavyweight boxing champion from 1952 to 1956, retiring undefeated.

11th Dec– American baseball legend Joe DiMaggio announced his retirement. He had played his final World Series game for the New York Yankees the day before.

Fashion Trends of the 1950s

With the misery and bleakness of the war years behind us, the 50s were a time to show off. Consumerism was now a way of life and we were all too willing to spend money on luxuries, non-essentials, and fashion.

How we looked and how we dressed became important everyday considerations for women and men. We spent money like never before, guided by our favorite fashion icons, and helped along by a maturing advertising industry which flooded us with fashion advice through newspapers, magazines, billboards, radio and television.

We know

what you want

and we have it

in the

College Shop—

Our campus shirt—smooth-finished, shirt-tailored cotton gabardine, 11.95
Our campus skirt—soft, wonderful cotton canvas with a web belt. Natural, black, dark green, rust, 14.95
The College Shop, Lord & Taylor
New York, Manhasset, Westchester, Millburn

Clothing manufacturers had perfected mass production techniques while providing military uniforms during the war years. They now shifted their focus to well made, stylish, ready-to-wear clothes.

National Bellas Hess catalog cover, 1951.

Le Petit Echo de la Mode cover, 29th April 1951.

The American Weekly cover, April 1950.

No longer just for the wealthy, the growing middle classes could now afford to be fashionable. Magazines and mail-order catalogs kept us informed of the latest trends in fashion, make-up, and accessories.

Dresses from the *National Bellas Hess* mail order catalog in a mix of
the "tea skirt" and "sheath" styles that were popular in the year 1951.

Mojud... the stocking with "Magic-Motion" in the knit for perfect fit.

These are the famous stockings that fit like a ballet dancer's tights because they're made for YOU IN MOTION. "Magic Motion" right in the knit, makes them "give" when you move, spring back when you stop! And because "Magic Motion" means perfect fit... Mojud stockings wear longer; look far more glamorous. No stress. No strain. No sagging. No bagging. No wonder women adore them!

"Magic Motion" makes Mojuds fit better...

Fashion Harmony colors. Proportioned leg sizes. Mojud-muted permanently dull finish. Stockings by Mojud, and there's lovely lingerie by Mojud, too.

Christian Dior's "New Look" from 1947.

As with before the war, all eyes looked to Paris for new directions in haute couture. In 1947 Christian Dior didn't disappoint, unveiling his glamorous, extravagant, ultra-feminine "New Look" to the world.

Gone were the boxy tailored jackets with padded shoulders and slim, short skirts. Paris had brought back femininity, with clinched waists, fuller busts and hips, and longer, wider skirts. The emphasis was on abundance. This New Look carried us for more than a decade, well into the 1950s.

The "New Look" in the early 50s.

To achieve this impossible hour-glass figure, corsets and girdles were sold in record numbers. Metal underwire bras made a comeback, and a new form of bra known as the "cathedral bra" or "bullet bra" became popular.

the very **least** we can do!

ve love to do wonderful
a things to make you feel small
I light and free as the air...little
gs like this, for example...o few inches

Early 50s bullet bra and girdle from Jantzen.

Catalog dresses from Spiegel's 1955 Spring-Summer Collection.

Nylons...Sweet 'n Fresh

Free-of-care nylon in fashions that stay crisp on hottest days, keep you cool 'n fresh always

Despite criticisms against the extravagance of the New Look, and arguments that heavy corsets and paddings undermined the freedoms women had won during the war years, the New Look was embraced on both sides of the Atlantic. Before long, inexpensive, ready-to-wear versions of Dior's New Look had found their way into our department store catalogs.

Dior also created a slimmed down alternative look, as a sleek dress or elegant straight skirt and short jacket. This groomed and tailored look, known as the sheath dress, continued to place emphasis on the hourglass figure.

Also known as the "wiggle dress", this sexier figure-hugging silhouette was preferred by movie stars such as Marilyn Monroe.

Women embraced the femininity of 1950s' fashion from head to toe. Hats, scarves, belts, gloves, shoes, stockings, handbags and jewelry were all given due consideration.

Out on the street, no outfit would be complete without a full complement of matching accessories.

FEELS SO GOOD. Fabrics made of acetate fiber are always comfortable because acetate always feels so soft and luxurious next to the skin.

IS ACETATE LIKE ANY OTHER FIBER? No. Acetate has a unique combination of qualities. It feels like silk. Washes with ease and dries quickly like nylon. But acetate has a beautiful, graceful drape that makes clothes hang exactly right and feel so good.

WHAT ACETATE IS. Acetate is the man-made textile fiber, cellulose acetate, pioneered by Celanese Corporation of America. Better fabrics of every description are made with this modern fiber.

STAYS SO FRESH. Suits and dresses of acetate stay fresh-looking. Because acetate fibers are naturally resilient they help fabrics shed their wrinkles after wearing. That's why acetate needs less pressing.

LAUNDERS SO EASILY. DRIES SO QUICKLY. Dirt washes off acetate with ease. Just a sudsing, a rinse, and your clothes are sparkling clean—ready to smooth on a hanger to dry. If preferred, press lightly with a moderate iron.

Is Acetate like any other fiber? No. Acetate has a unique combination of qualities. It feels like silk. Washes with ease and dries quickly like nylon. But acetate has a beautiful, graceful drape that makes clothes hang exactly right and feel so good.

What acetate is. Acetate is the man-made textile fiber, cellulose acetate, pioneered by Celanese Corporation of America. Better fabrics of every description are made with this modern fiber.

Feels so good. Fabrics made of acetate fiber are always comfortable because acetate always feels so soft and luxurious next to the skin.

Stays so fresh. Suits and dresses of acetate stay fresh-looking. Because acetate fibers are naturally resilient they help fabrics shed their wrinkles after wearing. That's why acetate needs less pressing.

Launders so easily. Dries so quickly. Dirt washes off acetate with ease. Just a sudsing, a rinse, and your clothes are sparkling clean–ready to smooth on a hanger to dry. If preferred, press lightly with a moderate iron.

Your snapshots say it best.

When you take snapshots of Dad, or Mother, or anyone dear to the whole family, think how much these would mean to others, far and near. Extra prints in your letters are the sure tie with family and friends–especially that boy in the Service.

This year... send Photo-Greeting Cards, made from your own snapshot. Order now from your dealer.

At your dealers–dependable Kodak and Brownie cameras for snapshot opportunities ahead. For black-and-white snapshots, Kodak Verichrome Film. For full-color snapshots, Kodacolor Film.

An Artificial Heart Machine October 1951

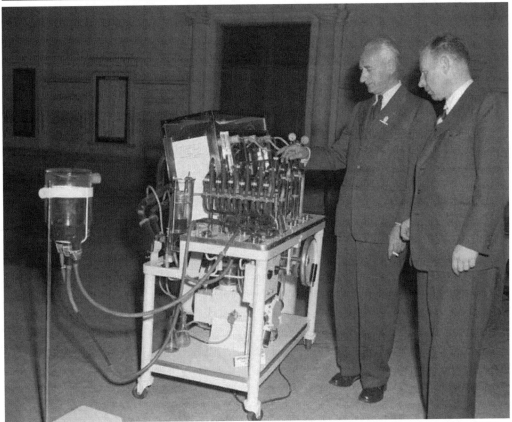

Professor Jacob Jongbloed (left) explains his artificial heart machine, 1951.

In October 1951, Professor Jacob Jongbloed from Utrecht, Holland, took to the floor at a meeting of the Congress of Surgeons, Sorbonne University in Paris, France. He presented his artificial heart machine, a mechanical heart replacement.

Long seen as the holy grail of medicine, the invention of the artificial heart machine could allow surgeons to perform life saving open heart surgery while the patient could be artificially kept alive.

The process was simple, blood would be diverted through the machine which would pump to circulate it back through the body. The patient's heart could be stopped during the period of operation.

Advances in cardiac procedures over the next few decades moved steadily. Artificial hearts and heart transplants, unimaginable back in the 1950s, are now commonplace.

Other News from 1951

19th-21st Jan– An unprecedented 649 avalanches in the Alps left a trail of destruction across Switzerland, Austria and Italy. Known as the "Winter of Terror", 40,000 people were buried under avalanche snow, with 265 deaths reported during the 3-month season.

3rd May– Royal Festival Hall opened as part of The Festival of Britain, a five-month national fair held in London, to promote science, technology, arts and culture.

Audience wearing 3D glasses view a stereoscopic film during the Festival of Britain.

8th May– America's first thermonuclear (hydrogen) bomb was tested at Enewetak Atoll in the new Pacific Proving Ground. This, and future tests, would pave the way for the first full scale thermonuclear bomb, tested in Nov 1952.

14th Jun– UNIVAC, (universal automated computer) became the first computer built for commercial purposes. At more than $1 million each, its relatively low cost and portability made it popular. First purchased by the United States Census Bureau, a total of 46 UNIVACs were sold by the maker Remington Rand.

20th Jul– King Abdullah I of Jordan was assassinated while attending Friday prayers in Jerusalem. The assassin, from the secret order "the Jihad", sought to prevent peace talks with Israel.

Just 96 hours earlier, a former Prime Minister of Lebanon had been assassinated for the same reason.

1st Sep– The United States, Australia and New Zealand signed a mutual defense pact known as the ANZUS Treaty. With a goal to protect the security of the Pacific, the pact has since unraveled with New Zealand and the US suspending their obligations to the Treaty.

4th Sep– The first coast to coast transmission was broadcast by CBS TV. Using state-of-the-art microwave technology, a speech delivered by President Truman in San Francisco was picked up by 87 stations in 47 cities. The speech focused on a US-Japan treaty that officially ended America's post-World War II occupation of Japan.

2nd Nov– 6,000 British troops arrived in Egypt to quell unrest in the Suez Canal. Increasing riots resulted in a state of emergency declared in Egypt the following month.

31st Dec– After distributing more than $13.3 billion in aid to rebuild Europe, the US put an end to the Marshall Plan. Also known as the European Recovery Program, the money was provided to reconstruct cities, industries and infrastructure heavily damaged during the war.

"My Food Budget bought the bouquet–Thanks to A&P!"

"Whoever coined that slogan, *"You can save more–more easily at A&P,"* really *has* something! There's no hunting out the best values from store to store. No comparing of quality and price each time you shop to make sure you're getting your money's worth for the prices asked. A&P's storewide values on hundreds of quality items *every day* let me shop at my convenience and enjoy savings, too. Not only that–I have confidence in everything I buy there, because A&P gives me my money back on any item I buy if I'm not *completely satisfied.* Why don't you "Test Shop" A&P? See how convenient it is to be able to buy everything you need at one store. See how much you save, too!"

Menus... All Good... Different, Too! It takes good food to make good meals–and your A&P has the widest selection of fine foods imaginable. You'll have no weekly "repeat performances" in your menus unless you prefer 'em!

See Your Savings... Check 'em, too! Prices stamped on every item at A&P show you what your spending as you shop... speed you through the checkout counter, too! Keep your cash-register slip, check and see your savings!

Give Your Food Dollars More Mileage! Remember... only about *one cent* of each dollar you spend at A&P goes for profit! Small profit is a good sign of big value... come see!

Now... Rainbow Hues to Accent Refrigerator Door Handles, *they're femineered!* Femineering at its finest–Pantry-Door shelves give convenient, front-row storage... full-width Freezers hold up to 50lbs... Coldstream Crispers keep vegetables and fruit fresher, longer... Stainless Steel Shelves... Egg-O-Mat, Diffuse-O-Lite, Shadowline styling and other great IH exclusives!

Famous in quality–*from top to bottom, inside and outside*–for excellent service year in, year out!

Seven models! Seven sizes! Seven prices!–to suit every family, every home, every budget. See all seven new beauties at your IH Refrigerator dealer's today.

Famous People Born in 1951

12th Jan– Kirstie Alley, American actress.

19th Jan– Martha Davis, American singer-songwriter (Motels).

23rd Jan– Chesley Sullenberger III, American pilot (Hudson River landing).

30th Jan– Phil Collins, English drummer & singer (Genesis).

10th Feb– Robert Iger, American entertainment exec. (CEO Walt Disney).

14th Feb– Kevin Keegan, English soccer forward & manager.

15th Feb– Jane Seymour, British actress.

20th Feb– Gordon Brown, British Prime Minister (2007-2010).

4th Mar– Chris Rea, English singer-songwriter.

14th Mar– Jerry Greenfield, American co-founder of Ben & Jerry's ice-cream.

17th Mar– Kurt Russell, American actor.

18th Mar– Ben Cohen, American co-founder of Ben & Jerry's ice-cream.

24th Mar– Pat Bradley, American golfer (6 LPGA major titles).

24th Mar– Tommy Hilfiger, American fashion designer.

6th Apr– Bert Blyleven, American Hall of Fame Baseball player.

10th Apr– Steven Seagal, American actor.

4th May– Jackie Jackson, American singer (Jackson 5).

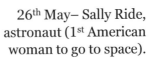

26th May– Sally Ride, astronaut (1st American woman to go to space).

5th June– Suze Orman, American financial advisor, writer, & television personality.

8th June– Bonnie Tyler, Welsh singer.

13th Jun– Stellan Skarsgård, Swedish actor.

3rd July– Jean-Claude Duvalier "Baby Doc", Haitian dictator-president (1971-1986).

6th July– Geoffrey Rush, Australian actor.

21st July– Robin Williams, American actor & comedian (d.2014).

5th Sep– Michael Keaton, American actor.

7th Sep– Chrissie Hynde, American singer-songwriter & guitarist (The Pretenders).

25th Sep– Mark Hamill, American actor (Luke Skywalker-Star Wars).

2nd Oct– Sting [Gordon Sumner], British singer-songwriter & bassist (The Police).

5th Oct– Bob Geldof, Irish singer (The Boomtown Rats) & activist (Live Aid).

7th Oct– John "Cougar" Mellencamp, American musician & actor.

14th Nov– Zhang Yimou, Chinese film director.

3rd Dec– Mike Stock, British songwriter, musician & record producer (Stock, Aitken & Waterman).

Help your child win success with the

World Book Encyclopedia

The extra advantages your child gets at home can mean the difference between success and failure in school and, later, in life. One proved way to give your child these vital advantages is by owning the remarkable World Book Encyclopedia.

Not only is the World Book first choice of America's schools and libraries, it is praised by thousands of parents as well.

In fact, 9 out of 10 parents report it has helped their children get better school marks in an amazingly short time.

Act now to discover the wonderful difference that owning the fascinating, easy-to-use World Book can make in your child's life. Find out, too, how much your whole family will enjoy World Book and gain benefits that can't be measured in money.

More World Books are purchased annually than any other encyclopedia in America

of America's schools and
libraries for more than 30 years
Ask any teacher or librarian

The extra advantage your child gets at home can mean the difference between success and failure in school and, later, in life. One proved way to give your child these vital advantages is by owning the remarkable World Book Encyclopedia.

Not only is the World Book first choice of America's schools and libraries, it is praised by thousands of parents as well. In fact, 9 out of 10 parents report it has helped their children get better school marks in an amazingly short time.

Act now to discover the wonderful difference that owning the fascinating easy-to-use World Book can make in your child's life. Find out, too, how much your whole family will enjoy World Book and gain benefits that can't be measured in money.

More World Books are purchased annually than any other encyclopedia in America.

1951 in Numbers

Census Statistics [1]:

- Population of the world — 2.58 billion
- Population in the United States — 160.8 million
- Population in the United Kingdom — 50.6 million
- Population in Canada — 14.08 million
- Population in Australia — 8.4 million
- Average age for marriage of women — 20.4 years old
- Average age for marriage of men — 22.9 years old
- USA divorce rate — 25 %
- Average family income USA — $3,700 per year
- Minimum wage USA — $0.75 per hour

Costs of Goods [2]:

- Average new house — $9,000
- Average new car — $1,500
- New Jaguar XK120 — $4,039
- A gallon of gas — $0.19
- Peanut butter — $0.28
- A loaf of bread — $0.18
- A gallon of milk — $0.92
- Hamburger meat — $0.50 per pound
- Frozen green beans — $0.48 per pound
- Sliced bacon — $0.55 per pound
- Eggs — $0.69 per dozen
- Rice — $0.17 per pound
- Cigarettes — $0.20 per pack
- Movie ticket — $0.47

[1] Figures taken from worldometers.info/world-population, US National Center for Health Statistics, *Divorce and Divorce Rates* US (cdc.gov/nchs/data/series/sr_21/sr21_029.pdf) and United States Census Bureau, *Historical Marital Status Tables* (census.gov/data/tables/time-series/demo/families/marital.html).
[2] Figures from thepeoplehistory.com and mclib.info/reference/local-history-genealogy/historic-prices/1951-2/.

Image Attributions

Photographs and images used in this book are reproduced courtesy of the following:

Page 4 – Advertisement from *Life* Magazine 12th Feb 1951. Source: books.google.com.sg/books?id=4EsEAAAAMBAJ& printsec. Pre 1978, no copyright mark (PD* image).
Page 6 – From the *LOOK* Magazine Photograph Collection. Source: Library of Congress, Prints & Photographs Division, [Reproduction number e.g., LC-L9-60-8812, frame 8]. (Public Domain (PD) image).
Page 7 – From the Benjamin Moore House Paint 1950s advertisement. Source: flickr.com/photos by 1950sUnlimited. Attribution 2.0 Generic (CC BY 2.0).
Page 8 – Bendix advertisement, source: books.google.com.sg/books?id=a1QEAAAAMBAJ& printsec. Pre 1978 (PD* image). – Magazine cover by Science Service Inc. Source: comicbookplus.com/?cbplus= atomic. Pre 1978, no mark (PD image).
Page 9 – Advertisement from *Life* Magazine 5th Mar 1951. Source: books.google.com.sg/books?id=0UsEAAAAMBAJ& printsec. Pre 1978, no copyright mark (PD* image).
Page 10 – Victoria Embankment j/w Westminster Bridge by Leonard Bentley. Source: search.creativecommons.org/ photos/3d631476-f436-4609-86b4-875edda5c618. License CC BY-SA 2.0 (PD image).
Page 11 – Creator unknown. Pre 1978, no copyright mark (PD image).
Page 12 – Advertisement from *Life* Magazine 5th Mar 1951. Source: books.google.com.sg/books?id=0UsEAAAAMBAJ& printsec. Pre 1978, no copyright mark (PD* image).
Page 13 – Photo source: dp.la. Photographer unknown, US government owned image (PD image).
Page 14 – Packard, source: books.google.com.sg/books?id=a1QEAAAAMBAJ&printsec. Pre 1978, no copyright mark (PD* image). – Studebaker, source: flickr.com/photos/andreboeni/30075178957/ by Andrew Bone. – Hudson, source: flickr.com/photos/andreboeni/26069330288/ by Andrew Bone. Attributions 4.0 International (CC BY 4.0).
Page 15 & 16 – Advertisements from *Life* Magazine 9th Apr & 12th Mar 1951. Source: books.google.com.sg/books?id= 4E4EAAAAMBAJ&printsec & books.google.com.sg/books?id=x0sEAAAAMBAJ& printsec. Pre 1978 (PD* image).
Page 17 – Advertisements from *Life* Magazine 1st Oct and 3rd Dec 1951. Source: books.google.com.sg/books?id=a1QEAAAA MBAJ&printsec and books.google.com.sg/books?id=oVQEAAAAMBAJ&printsec. Pre 1978, no copyright mark (PD* image).
Page 18 – *The Colgate Comedy Hour, by Colgate-Palmolive-Peet.* Source: commons.wikimedia.org/wiki/File:Dean_Martin_ Jerry_Lewis_Colgate_Comedy_Hour_early_1950s.JPG. Pre 1978, no copyright mark (PD image).
–*The Lone Ranger* promotional photo from ABC Television April 11, 1960. Pre 1978, no copyright mark (PD image).
Page 19 – *Dragnet* by NBC, still image from Season 1, Episode 2. – *Search for Tomorrow*, by CBS.
Source: imdb.com/title/tt0043229/mediaviewer/ rm1990866176. – Promotional photo for *The Red Skelton Show,* by NBC. – *Crazy People,* BBC 1951. Source: bbc.co.uk/comedy/thegoonshow/. Images this page are reproduced in low-resolution for information only under fair use terms. It is believed that these images will not devalue the ability of the copyright holder to profit from the original works.
Page 20 – Advertisement from *Life* Magazine 4th Jun 1951. Source: books.google.com.sg/books?id=b1EEAAAAMBAJ& printsec. Pre 1978, no copyright mark (PD* image).
Page 21 – Screen still from *I Love Lucy,* by CBS Broadcasting, taken from the book *I Love Lucy: Celebrating 50 years of Love and Laughter,* by Elisabeth Edwards, Running Press Book Publishers, 2010. Source: Library of Congress (097.01.00). [Digital ID # lucy0097_02]. (PD image). – Still Image from *I Love Lucy,* 14th Nov 1955 episode "Face to Face". Source: wikipedia.org/ wiki/I_Love_Lucy#/media/File:I_Love_Lucy_1955.JPG. Courtesy of Desilu and CBS Broadcasting, Inc. (PD image).
– Publicity photo of the *I Love Lucy* cast by CBS Broadcasting. Source: commons.wikimedia.org/wiki/Category:Lucille_Ball#/ media/File:I_Love_Lucy_Cast.JPG. Pre 1978, no copyright mark (PD image).
Page 22 – Advertisement from *Life* Magazine 5th Feb 1951. Source: books.google.com.sg/books?id=50sEAAAAMBAJ& printsec. Pre 1978, no copyright mark (PD* image).
Page 23 – US tank and crew, source: commons.wikimedia.org/wiki/File:HA-SC-98-06983-Crew_of_M24_along_Naktong_ River_front-Korean_war-17_Aug_1950.JPEG. Camera Operator: SGT. RILEY. – Infantrymen behind tank, source: commons.wikimedia.org/wiki/Korean_War from the U.S. National Archives and Records Administration. Images this page are US Federal Government owned (PD image).
Page 24 – F4U-4B Corsair from the Air and Space Museum No. 306-FS-237-2 - U.S. Defenselmagery photo VIRIN: HD-SN-98-07598. Source: commons.wikimedia.org/wiki/Korean_War#/media/File:F4U-4B_VF-113_CV-47_1950.JPEG. – Hawker Sea Fury (This photograph was released by Commander, Naval Forces Far East on 7 June 1951) No. NH 97044. Source: commons.wikimedia.org/wiki/Korean_War#/media/File:SeaFury_launch.jpg. – Fighter bomber USAF - U.S. Defense Imagery photo VIRIN: HD-SN-98-07611. Source: commons.wikimedia.org/wiki/Korean_War#/media/File:P51_Mustang_ bombs_NKorea_HD-SN-98-07611.jpeg. All images this page are property of the US Army, Federal Government (PD images).
Page 25 – Medical corpsmen, 1st Battalion Aid Station, 31st Infantry Regiment, 7th U.S. Infantry Division. Photo #1-4885-4/FEC-52-30954 (Sylvester). Source: commons.wikimedia.org/wiki/ File:Medical-corpsmen-korea.jpg.
– US soldiers photo source: commons.wikimedia.org/wiki/File:KoreanWarFallenSoldier1.jpg. – Korean girl carrying baby brother, by Maj. R.V. Spencer, UAF (Navy). Source: commons.wikimedia.org/wiki/File: KoreanWarRefugee WithBaby.jpg, from the National Archives & Records Administration, cataloged under National Archives Identifier (NAID) 520796. All images this page are property of the US Army, owned by the Federal Government (PD images).
Page 26 – Advertisement from *Life* Magazine 14th May 1951. Source: books.google.com.sg/books?id=jlEEAAAAMBAJ& printsec. Pre 1978, no copyright mark (PD* image).
Page 27 – Nuclear explosion 1951, courtesy of National Nuclear Security Administration. Source: en.wikipedia.org/wiki/ Nevada_Test_Site. Property of US Federal Government (PD image). – Las Vegas postcard, 1951. Source: mensonges.fr/ bombe/bombe.html. Pre 1978, no copyright mark (PD* image).
Page 28 – Rosenbergs by Roger Higgins, source: loc.gov/resource/cph.3c17772/ Library of Congress (PD image).
Page 29 – Churchill with Randolf Churchill & Winston Spencer-Churchill, from the Library of Congress Toni Frissell Collection: LC-DIG-ppmsca-0537. Copyright released (PD image). – Churchill with Eisenhower & Montgomery, by ACME Newspictures, in the Library of Congress NY World-Telegram & Sun Collection, copyright released (PD image).
Page 30 – Advertisement from *Life* Magazine 3rd Dec 1951. Source: books.google.com.sg/books?id=oVQEAAAAMBAJ& printsec. Pre 1978, no copyright renewal (PD* image).
Page 31 – PLA in Lhasa, author 《解放军报》记者. Source: commons.wikimedia.org/wiki/File:PLA_marching_into_Lhasa. jpg. Pre 1978, no copyright mark (PD image). – Dalai Lama, source: commons.wikimedia.org/wiki/File:Dalai_Lama_in_ 1956_in_New_Delhi.jpg by Kinsey Brothers. (PD image India).
Page 32 – Danger Sign, reproduction of a farm sign in Johannesburg. 1st July 1952. Source: commons.wikimedia.org/wiki/ Category:Apartheid_signage (PD image). – Photo from timeslive.co.za, photographer unknown. (PD image).
Page 33 – Photo from sahistory.org.za, photographer unknown. Pre 1978, no copyright mark (PD image).
– Photo from religiousleftlaw.com, photographer unknown. Pre 1978, no copyright mark (PD image).
Page 34 – Advertisement from Life Magazine 9th Apr 1951. Source: books.google.com.sg/books?id=4E4EAAAAMBAJ& printsec. Pre 1978, no copyright mark (PD* image).
Page 35 – Advertisement from *Life* Magazine 12th Nov 1951. Source: books.google.com.sg/books?id=fFQEAAAAMBAJ& printsec. Pre 1978, no copyright renewal (PD* image).

Page 36 – Scene from *Quo Vadis* trailer, by MGM 1951. Source: en.wikipedia.org/wiki/Quo_Vadis_(1951_film)#/media/ File:Quo_Vadis_(1951)_trailer_8.jpg. (PD image). – Still image from video of *The Redbook Awards*, 1953.
– Publicity photo of Grace Kelly in 1951, on the set of *High Noon*, by United Artists. Non-PD images this page are low-resolution images for information only, reproduced under fair use terms. It is believed that these images will not devalue the ability of the copyright holders to profit from the original works.
Page 37 – *An American in Paris*, 1951 film poster by MGM. – *The African Queen*, 1951 film poster by United Artist Corp. Source: en.wikipedia.org/wiki/The_African_Queen_(film). – *Quo Vadis*, 1951 film poster by MGM. Copyright for movie posters, where not Public Domain, are possibly owned by either the publisher or the creator of the work depicted. Images included this page are for information only under US fair use laws. The images are low resolution copies too small to be used to make illegal copies for another book. These images will not limit the copyright owner's rights to sell the products.
Page 38 – The Day the Earth Stood Still, 1951 movie poster by 20th Century Fox. Source: en.wikipedia.org/wiki/The_Day_ the_Earth_Stood_Still (PD image). – The Man from Planet X, 1951 movie poster by United Artists. Source: en.wikipedia. org/wiki/The_Man_from_Planet_X. – Flight to Mars, 1951 movie poster by Monogram. Source: en.wikipedia.org/wiki/ Flight_to_Mars_(film). – When Worlds Collide, 1951 movie poster by Paramount. Source: en.wikipedia.org/wiki/When_ Worlds_Collide_(1951_film). Copyright for movie posters, where not Public Domain, are possibly owned by either the publisher or the creator of the work depicted. Images included this page are for information only under US fair use laws. The images are low resolution copies too small to make illegal copies for another book. These images will not limit the copyright owner's rights to sell the products in any way.
Page 39 –Vivien Leigh, source: en.wikipedia.org/wiki/A_Streetcar_Named_Desire_(1951_film). Pre 1978, no copyright mark (PD image). – Cinema poster from 1951. Source: en.wikipedia.org/wiki/. Pre 1978, no copyright renewal (PD image). – Portrait of Marlon Brando in the theatre production of *A Streetcar Named Desire*, 27th Dec 1948. From the Library of Congress, Van Vechten Collection. Source: en.wikipedia.org/wiki/A_Streetcar_Named_Desire#/media/File:Van_Vechten_ Marlon_Brando_image_170904.jpg (PD image).
Page 40 – Advertisement from *Life* Magazine 9th Apr 1951. Source: books.google.com.sg/books?id=4E4EAAAAMBAJ& printsec. Pre 1978, no copyright mark (PD* image).
Page 41 – Advertisement from *Life* Magazine 5th Nov 1951. Source: books.google.com.sg/books?id=gFQEAAAAMBAJ& printsec. Pre 1978, no copyright mark (PD* image).
Pages 42 & 43 – Rogers and Hammerstein 1945 press photo, Source: commons.wikimedia.org/wiki/File:Rodgers_and_ Hammerstein_at_piano-original.jpg (PD image). – Brynner portrait by CBS, 1972. Source: en.wikipedia.org/wiki/File:Yul_ Brynner_Anna_and_the_King_television_1972.JPG (PD image). All other images this page available by creative commons, source: en.wikipedia.org/wiki/The_King_and_I. Pre 1978, no copyright mark (PD image).
Page 44 – Nat King Cole in 1952 by GAC-General Artists Corporation (management). Permission PD-PRE1978 (PD image). – Tony Bennett in the 50s, source: en.wikipedia.org/wiki/Tony_Bennett. Pre 1978, no mark (PD image). – Perry Como by NBC Television, 1956. Source: commons.wikimedia.org/wiki/File:Perry_Como_1956. Permission PD-PRE1978 (PD image). – Patti Page source: wikivisually.com/wiki/Patti_Page by General Artists Corporation.Permission PD-PRE1978 (PD image).
Page 45 – Shore promotional photo by Paramount, 1951. Source: en.wikipedia.org/wiki/Dinah_Shore (PD image).
– Reynolds photo by Bob Beerman, 1954. Source: en.wikipedia.org/wiki/Debbie_Reynolds. (PD image).
Page 46 – Advertisement from *Life* Magazine 3rd Sep 1951. Source: books.google.com.sg/books?id=k04EAAAAMBAJ& printsec. Pre 1978, no copyright mark (PD* image).
Page 47 – Roubanis lighting the torch, 25th Feb 1951. source: commons.wikimedia.org/wiki/File:Panamericanos.jpg. Pre 1978, no copyright renewal (PD image). – Poster source: en.wikipedia.org/wiki/File:Pan_am_1951.jpg.
– Magazine cover, source: guides.library.illinois.edu/sports. Poster and magazine images are possibly owned by creator. Images are for information only, included under US fair use laws. The images are low resolution, too small to make illegal copies for another book. These will not limit the owner's rights to sell the products in any way.
Page 48 – Advertisement from *Life* Magazine 5th Mar 1951. Source: books.google.com.sg/books?id=0UsEAAAAMBAJ& printsec. Pre 1978 (PD* image).
Page 49 – Hogan in a homecoming parade on Broadway, photo 21st July 1953 by Dick DeMarsico. Source: loc.gov/pictures/ resource/cph.3c15559/ rep number LC-USZ62-115559. (PD image). – Connolly in 1953, from the Dutch National Archives, source: commons.wikimedia.org/wiki/Category:Maureen_Connolly#/media/File:Maureen_ Connolly_1953.jpg (PD image). – Chadwick press photo in 1951. Source: commons.wikimedia.org/wiki/Category: Florence_Chadwick#/media/File: Florence_Chadwick_1951.jpg. Pre 1978, no copyright renewal (PD image). – DiMaggio in a 1951 issue of Baseball Digest. Source: commons.wikimedia.org/wiki/Category:Joe_DiMaggio#/ media/File:Joe_DiMaggio_1951.png (PD image).
Page 50 – Advertisement for Lord and Taylor. Pre 1978, no copyright mark (PD image).
Page 51 – Fashion magazine covers from 1951. Pre 1978, no copyright mark (PD image).
Page 52 – Advertisement source: imgur.com/gallery/F6UwKM2. Pre 1978, no copyright mark (PD image).
Page 53 – From *Life* Mag 12th Mar 1951. Source: books.google.com.sg/books?id=x0sEAAAAMBAJ& printsec. (PD* image).
Page 54 – Photo by Lars Nordin, CC BY 4.0, Source: commons.wikimedia.org/w/index.php?curid=39208366
Page 55 – Jantzen advert. Source: flickr.com/photos/nesster/5521936717/ Attribution 4.0 International (CC BY 4.0)
Page 56 – Marilyn Monroe in 1952 studio publicity portrait for film Niagara, by 20th Century Fox. (PD image).
– Models walking photo. Source: Jessica at myvintagevogue.com. Licensed under CC BY 2.0.
Page 57 & 58 – Advertisements from *Life* Magazine 12th Nov & 8th Oct 1951. Sources: books.google.com.sg/books?id= fFQEAAAAMBAJ&printsec and books.google.com.sg/books?id=jFQEAAAAMBAJ&printsec. Pre 1978 (PD* image).
Page 59 – Jongbloed, 30th August 1951. Source unknown. Pre 1978, no copyright mark (PD image).
Page 60 – At the Telekinema, Festival of Britain 11th May 1951, from The National Archives UK record WORK25/208. Source: en.wikipedia.org/wiki/File:The_National_Archives_UK_-_WORK_25-208.jpg. Pre 1978, no copyright mark (PD image). – Greenhouse George nuclear test, 9th May 1951. From the National Nuclear Security Administration. Source: en.wikipedia.org/wiki/Operation_Greenhouse. US Federal Government photo (PD image).
Page 61 – Truman, 16th Dec 1950, from the National Archives and Records Administration (NAID) 541951. Source: en.wikipedia.org/wiki/Presidency_of_Harry_S._Truman. US Federal Government photo (PD image). – Egypt, screen still taken from video *Egypt Crisis* by Brithish Pathe. Source: youtube.com/watch?v=-zOlcHiBl9c reproduced under Fair Use laws, being low resolution and too small to make illegal copies. This will not limit the owner's rights to sell the products.
Page 62 & 63 – Advertisements from *Life* Magazine 9th July & 5th Mar 1951. Sources: books.google.com.sg/books?id= m04EAAAAMBAJ&printsec & books.google.com.sg/books?id=0UsEAAAAMBAJ&printsec. Pre 1978 (PD* image).
Page 64 & 65 – All photos are, where possible, CC BY 2.0 or PD images made available by the creator for free use including commercial use. Where commercial use photos are unavailable, photos are included here for information only under US fair use laws due to: 1- images are low resolution copies; 2- images do not devalue the ability of the copyright holders to profit from the original works in any way; 3- Images are too small to be used to make illegal copies for use in another book; 4- The images are relevant to the article created.
Page 66 – Advertisement from *Life* Magazine 1st Oct 1951. Source: books.google.com.sg/books?id=a1QEAAAAMBAJ& printsec. Pre 1978, no copyright mark (PD* image).

*Advertisements (or images from an advertisements) published in a collective work (such as a magazine or periodical issue) in the United States between 1925 and 1977,and without a valid and current copyright notice specific to the advertisements, have fallen into the public domain under current USA copyright laws.

These words first appeared in print in the year 1951.

cargo pants

GUNPOINT

patented

Manic-depressive illness

acrylic fiber

genetic engineering

cable television

White Nationalist

Murphy's Law

slippery slope

hydroxychloroquine

WRAP-UP

whiteboard

teleprompter

FAST-FOOD

SUPPORT GROUP

trailblazing

*From merriam-webster.com/time-traveler/1951.

Please help me out:

I sincerely hope you enjoyed reading this book and that it brought back many fond memories from the past.

I have enjoyed researching and writing this book for you and would greatly appreciate your feedback by way of a written review and/or star rating.

First and foremost, I am always looking to grow and improve as a writer. It is reassuring to hear what works, as well as to receive constructive feedback on what could improve.

Second, starting out as an unknown author is exceedingly difficult, and Customer Reviews go a long way toward making the journey out of anonymity possible.

Please help me by taking a few moments to leave a review for others to read.

Best regards,
Bernard Bradforsand-Tyler.

Please leave a
book review/rating at:

http://bit.ly/1951reviews

Or scan the QR code:

Made in the USA
Middletown, DE
21 May 2021

40182197R00040